The Nature Kid's Guide to
CRABS

DAVID ANDERSON

LP Media Inc. Publishing
Text copyright © 2026 by LP Media Inc.
All rights reserved.

For information address LP Media Inc. Publishing,
30012 Variolite St NW, Princeton MN 55371
www.lpmedia.org

Publication Data

Crabs
The Nature Kid's Guide to Crabs — First edition.

Summary: "Learn all about Crabs, the Nature Kid Way"
— Provided by publisher.

ISBN: 979-8-89818-192-5

[1. Crabs – Non-Fiction] I. Title.

Title: The Nature Kid's Guide to Crabs

CONTENTS

CRAB HANGOUTS

A group of crabs is called a cast, just like actors in a play or movie!

Click, clack! A blue crab runs sideways across the wet sand.

Crabs are amazing animals with hard shells and strong claws. They come in many shapes and sizes. There are more than 4,500 kinds of crabs on Earth!

You can find crabs on sandy beaches and in deep seas. Some even live on land or up in trees! These tough creatures make their homes in many surprising places.

Crabs walk sideways to move fast. Their legs bend in a way that makes scooting left and right easy. Watch a crab on the sand and you will see it zip along like a tiny race car!

SHELL SECRETS

Crack! A dungeness crab splits its old shell and wiggles free.

A crab wears its bones on the outside! This hard cover is called an **exoskeleton**. It keeps the soft body safe inside like a suit of armor.

As a crab grows, its shell gets too tight. The crab must molt. It breaks out of the old shell and grows a new one. The new shell starts off soft and squishy.

During this time, the crab hides while its shell gets hard. This can take a few days. Once the shell is firm, the crab is ready to explore again.

Some crabs molt more than 20 times before they are fully grown. Each new shell is bigger than the last!

CLAW CRAFT

A coconut crab's claws can squeeze with as much force as a lion's bite!

Crunch! A fiddler crab cracks open a snail shell with one big claw.

A crab's claws are some of the strongest tools in the ocean. They can crack open hard shells, tear apart food, and grip onto rocks in a rushing current. Claws do it all.

When two crabs fight, those claws become weapons. They push, grab, and wrestle until one backs down. The crab with the bigger, stronger claws usually wins.

The most amazing part? If a crab loses a claw in a fight, it can grow a whole new one. Each time the crab **molts** and sheds its shell, the new claw gets a little bigger.

CRAB CRUSADERS

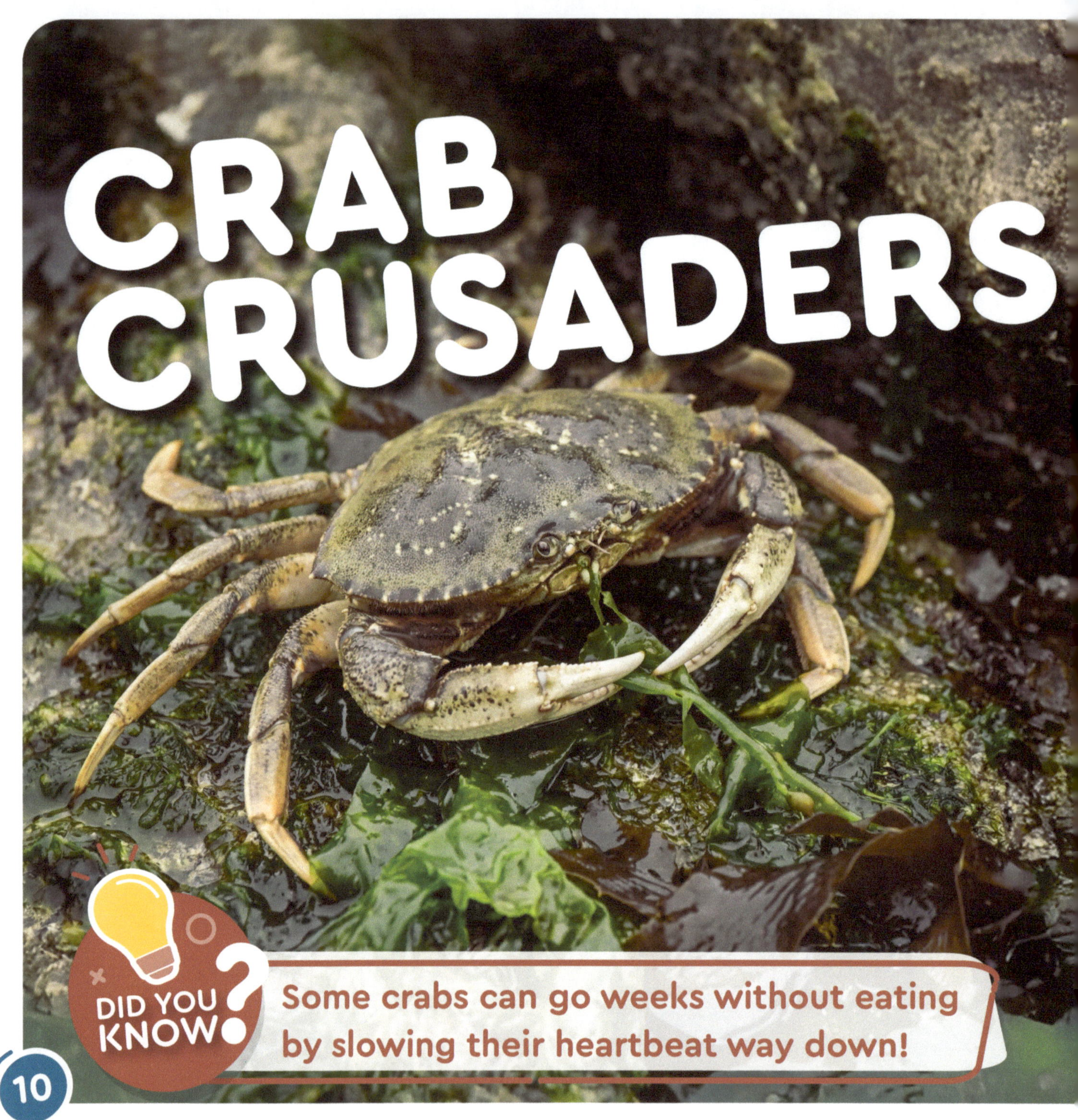

Munch! A crab chomps on some seaweed in a rocky tide pool.

Crabs eat many kinds of food. They munch on plants, worms, and small fish. Some crabs even eat dead animals on the sea floor, helping keep the ocean clean.

Most crabs make their homes near the sea. They tuck into cracks in rocks or coral. But other crabs live in fresh water like rivers and streams.

Crabs are most active at night. They come out to look for food in the dark. By morning, they are back in their hiding spots, resting until the sun goes down again.

SHELL SWAPPERS

Pop! A hermit crab squeezes into a brand new spiral shell.

Hermit crabs do not grow their own shells. Instead, they find empty snail shells and move right in. They carry their shells everywhere they go, and a good shell keeps them safe from hungry birds and fish.

When a hermit crab gets too big for its shell, it goes looking for a bigger one. Sometimes crabs line up by size to swap shells! The biggest one picks first, then each crab moves into the next shell down the line.

Hermit crabs live on beaches and in shallow water all over the world. See if you can spot one on your next trip to the ocean!

HUGE CLAWS

14

Clap! A fiddler crab waves its giant claw high up in the air.

Fiddler crabs are easy to spot. Males have one tiny claw and one huge claw. The big claw can be half the size of their whole body!

Male fiddler crabs wave their big claw to attract a mate. They move it up and down like a fiddle player making music. That is how they got their name.

These small crabs live in muddy marshes and sandy shores. They dig **burrows** up to two feet deep to stay cool and safe from waves. At low tide, they come out to eat tiny plants and bits of dead animals.

BLUE BATTLERS

Splash! A blue crab paddles through the water with flat back legs.

Blue crabs live along the coast of North America. They are named for their bright blue claws. Their shells can be green or brown on top, helping them blend in with murky water.

Blue crabs are strong swimmers. Their back legs are shaped like paddles. They glide through bays and rivers looking for clams and fish to eat.

These crabs are fierce fighters. They snap at anything that comes too close. Even other blue crabs better watch out for those powerful claws!

Blue crabs can swim about three times faster than they can walk!

GHOSTLY GALLOP

Ghost crabs make a growling sound by grinding their stomach teeth to scare off enemies!

Zip! A Ghost crab races across the moonlit beach in a flash.

Ghost crabs are named for their pale color. Their sandy colored skin helps them hide on the beach. You might walk right past one and never see it!

These crabs are super fast. They can run up to 10 miles per hour, making them one of the fastest crabs on land. Their long legs help them zoom across the sand.

Ghost crabs come out mostly at night. They dig burrows up to four feet deep near the water. During the day, they rest inside their sandy tunnels, safe from the hot sun.

LIVING FOSSILS

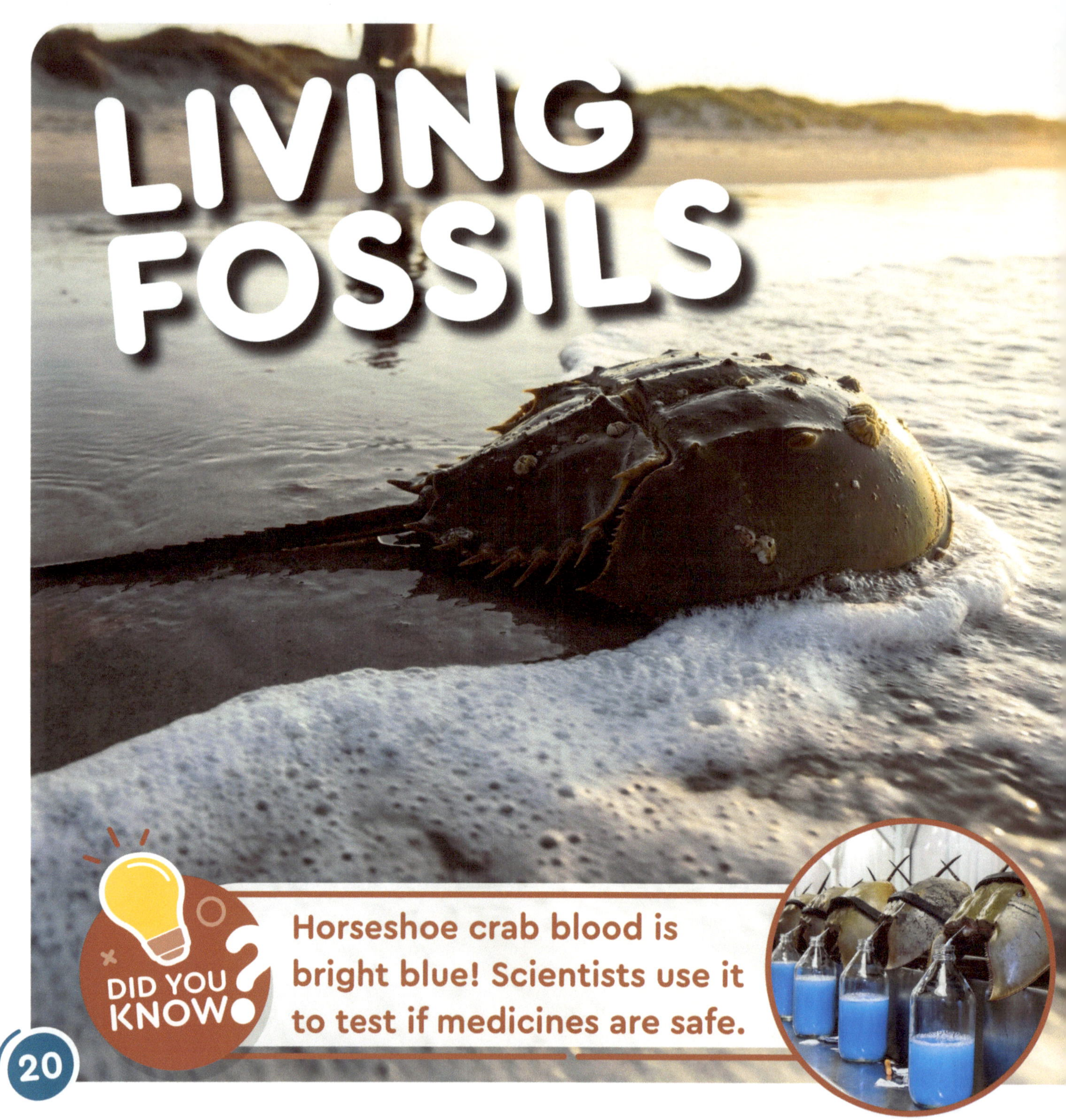

Horseshoe crab blood is bright blue! Scientists use it to test if medicines are safe.

20

Swoosh! A horseshoe crab crawls out of the surf onto the sand.

Horseshoe crabs are not really crabs at all! They are closer to spiders and scorpions. These odd animals have been around for over 450 million years. That is older than the dinosaurs!

A horseshoe crab has a big round shell and a long pointy tail. The tail is not a weapon. It helps the crab flip over if a wave knocks it on its back.

Every spring, horseshoe crabs come to the shore to lay eggs. Thousands arrive at the same time. Hungry birds flock to the beach to feast on the tiny green eggs.

KING CRABS

FUN FACT!
A red king crab can weigh up to 24 pounds. That's as big as some dogs!

Thud! A king crab drops onto the cold ocean floor far below.

King crabs are some of the biggest crabs in the sea. The red king crab can stretch six feet from claw to claw. That is as wide as a grown-up is tall!

These crabs live in cold, deep water near Alaska. They walk slowly along the ocean floor, sometimes 600 feet below the surface. They use their strong legs to find food in the mud.

King crabs eat worms, clams, and small sea stars. Their thick shells are covered in sharp bumps and spines. This armor helps keep hungry fish away.

COCONUT CRUSHERS
DID YOU KNOW?
Coconut crabs can live for over 60 years, twice as long as hermit crabs!
24

Smash! A coconut crab breaks open a coconut with one mighty snap.

Coconut crabs are the biggest land crabs in the world. They can grow up to three feet wide and weigh nine pounds. Their claws are so strong they can crack open coconuts!

These crabs are a type of hermit crab. But as adults, they do not need a shell. Their bodies grow a tough outer layer instead.

Coconut crabs live on islands in the Indian and Pacific oceans. They climb trees to grab fruit and coconuts using their powerful legs. Their sense of smell is amazing. They can sniff out a ripe coconut or a piece of fruit from over a mile away!

SPIDER GIANTS

Whoosh! A giant spider crab stretches its long legs on the deep sea floor.

The Japanese spider crab is the biggest crab in the world. Its legs can span over 12 feet from tip to tip. That is wider than a car!

This crab lives deep in the ocean near Japan. It crawls along the sea floor on its long, thin legs, eating dead fish and plants it finds down there.

Even though it looks scary, this crab is gentle. Its legs may be long, but its body is only about 15 inches wide. It moves slowly and quietly through the deep, dark water.

DISGUISE DESIGNER

Plop! A tiny crab sticks bits of seaweed all over its bumpy shell.

Decorator crabs are the artists of the sea. They stick bits of seaweed, sponges, and even tiny animals onto their shells.

This clever **camouflage** helps them blend in with the ocean floor. Hungry fish swim right past without seeing them!

When a decorator crab molts, it loses its disguise and starts all over again. Some crabs even move decorations from their old shell to the new one. Talk about recycling!

FUN FACT!

Some decorator crabs stick stinging sea creatures on their shells!

POM POM CRABS

Swish, swish! A tiny crab waves two little sea anemones like pom poms.

Pom pom crabs are very small. They are only about one inch wide. But they have a clever trick that makes them special.

These crabs hold tiny sea **anemones** in each claw. Sea anemones can sting! The crab waves them at anything that tries to attack. It looks like a cheerleader with pom poms!

The anemones get something out of the deal too. As the crab eats, the anemones catch tiny bits of floating food. Both animals help each other survive. That is what teamwork looks like in the ocean!

RED TIDE MARCHERS

DID YOU KNOW?

Christmas Island red crabs can travel up to five miles on their march to the sea, and some trips take over a week!

Crunch! Millions of bright red crabs march across a road toward the sea.

Every year, millions of Christmas Island red crabs leave their forest homes and march to the ocean. The whole island turns red as up to 50 million crabs cover roads, bridges, and yards. People even close roads to let them pass!

The crabs make this long trip to lay their eggs in the sea. Mothers drop their eggs into the waves, and the ocean carries the babies away. Weeks later, tiny baby crabs crawl back onto land.

The people of Christmas Island build special bridges and tunnels just for the crabs. The little red travelers squeeze through fences and never stop until they reach the water!

TINY BEGINNINGS

Swirl! Thousands of tiny crab babies float through the ocean like specks of dust.

Most crabs start life as tiny larvae floating in the ocean. They look nothing like crabs at all. They are see-through specks with long spines, drifting with the waves.

As they grow, the larvae change shape many times. Slowly they start to look more like real crabs. Finally, they sink to the ocean floor and begin their life as a crawling crab.

A mother crab can carry thousands of eggs tucked under her belly. When the eggs are ready, she releases them into the sea. From that moment, the tiny babies are on their own!

OCEAN BALANCE

Splish! A fisherman tosses a crab back into the sea. It needs to grow a bit more!

People have caught crabs for food for thousands of years. Fishers use traps to bring in crabs from the sea. Blue crabs and Dungeness crabs are two popular types to eat.

But too much fishing can hurt crab numbers. Pollution and trash in the water also cause harm. When the ocean gets too warm, it can be hard for crabs to survive and grow.

Many people work to protect crabs today. They make rules about how many crabs can be caught. Cleaning up beaches and oceans helps crabs stay healthy for years to come.

CRAB SPOTTERS

Crash! A blue crab is washed up on shore by a wave.

Next time you are at the beach, take a closer look. That empty shell might have a hermit crab inside. That tiny hole in the sand could be a ghost crab's front door. Crabs are everywhere if you know where to look.

From the giant spider crab deep in the ocean to the tiny pom pom crab waving its anemones, every crab has its own amazing way of living. They crack, climb, swim, dig, and even grow back body parts!

So grab a bucket, head to the nearest tide pool, and see what is scurrying around. Your own crab adventure is waiting!

GLOSSARY

exoskeleton
The hard outer shell that protects a crab's soft body.

molt
To shed an old shell so a new, bigger one can grow.

camouflage
Colors or patterns that help an animal blend in and hide.

burrow
A hole or tunnel dug in sand or mud for shelter.

anemone
A soft sea animal that sticks to rocks and can sting.